The 30 Second Elephant and the Paper Airplane Experiment

written and illustrated by
DANIEL STILLMAN

PUBLISHED BY THE CONVERSATION FACTORY
COPYRIGHT © DANIEL STILLMAN 2018

The People Who Pushed Me

Although it's all a butterfly effect, this book wouldn't exist without just a very few people, in this chronological order:

My father took me to the Museum of Natural History when I was 6 to learn origami underneath the holiday tree there. He cultivated my enthusiasm for the craft and folded with me. Years later he showed me that I could solve my own problems faster than he could.

My mother bought me all the origami paper and books I ever wanted (within reason) and it was her friend Stephen who introduced me to Michael. She also somehow convinced my dad that it was a good idea to let me cut school for a few days to help volunteer for the origami convention set ups each year. She also convinced my dad to let our Jewish family get a Christmas tree so I could cover it in origami!

Michael was the most generous teacher and friend and he gave me a wealth of lessons I'm still absorbing.

Miles, who said yes to the crazy idea of design thinking for non-designers. I had no idea it would be a thing.

My cousin Jeremy Redleaf, whose Cave Day event series gave me the time to sit down and draw a first draft of this crazy book.

Carl, who said I was a charlatan for years, and almost made me believe it. He also asked me to make something from inside myself, at 100%.

This is not that book...but it's a prototype for it!

TABLE OF CONTENTS

Chapter Zero
Why This Book Exists   6

Chapter One
Blind Origami   17

Chapter Two
The Paper Airplane Experiment   27

Chapter Three
The 30 Second Elephant   39

Chapter Four
Make, Test, Reflect   51

Chapter Five
Final Thoughts   60

CHAPTER ZERO

WHY THIS BOOK EXISTS

This is a book about origami and mastering design thinking. Why on earth would anyone write such an odd book? This book exists mainly as a result of the influence of Michael Shall. He took me on as his origami sidekick when I was 13 and showed me how to keep an audience of any size in thrall, how to make things clear, and how to keep friends. He showed me these things and I'm still learning them, all these years later!

I'm going to tell you a little about my journey with origami. Don't worry! It's all going to tie together.

My mentor Michael was one of the first full-time origami professionals in the US. When he passed away at the all-too-young age of 45, he rated an obit in the New York Times, which described him as "a leading American expert in origami." He taught at schools and museums, including the American Museum of Natural History, the Cooper-Hewitt Museum, the Museum of Modern Art, and the Smithsonian Institution in Washington. And I was lucky enough to get to scurry along after him carrying his bags.

If you've ever been to NYC during the holidays, you might have seen his origami Christmas trees. He was responsible for the "Origami Holiday Tree" at the Museum of Natural History that's still going to this day (and the actual site where I first learned origami!) In the 90's, his "Paper Magic on Fifth Avenue" for

Japan Airlines was a sight to behold. And a bear to take down... he recruited a small gang of origami enthusiasts to help him dismantle it at the end of the season. It took me a few years to realize why it was so challenging...Michael was left handed and all the wires attaching the models to the fake tree were twisted in the opposite direction from what you'd expect.

Watching him teach was like a high-wire act with no net: just grit and pure energy. He also introduced me to paperfolding luminaries like Akira Yoshizawa, David Lister, Robert Lang, John Montroll, Tomoko Fuse, and Peter Engel. For me, paperfolding wasn't just a pastime, it was a window into deep secrets about the nature of the world. When I read Peter Engel's book, *Origami from Angelfish to Zen* at 14, it taught me about fractals, evolution, and literally dreaming your way into solutions. It was more than a hobby, it was an obsession.

One of the cool things about origami is how global it has become. The luminaries I listed include Japanese experts (where the artform flourished first) as well as American and British talents. I can pick up an origami book from anywhere in the world and work out the models explained inside. That's because of a universal language of origami co-developed by Akira Yoshizawa and Sam Randlett in the 60s.

Yoshizawa-Randlett Origami Notation

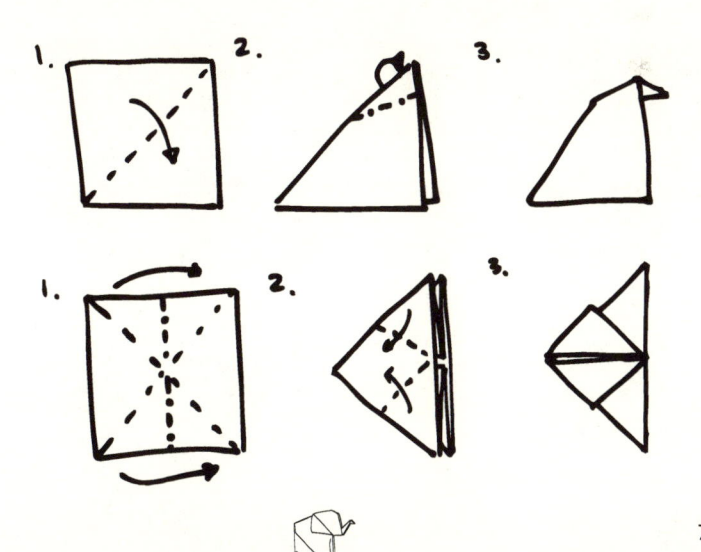

When I got into the world of user experience design years later, I noticed the similarities between the Yoshizawa- Randlett standard origami notation and the wireframe sketching style used commonly in user experience design to draw websites and mobile apps. Visual explanation is universal, (I reasoned) and so I offered a series of workshops on origami sketching back in 2011 both to my design team at Kaleidoscope as well as to other willing agencies like Method and groups like VizThink NYC. It was fun and insightful to cross these two worlds. The designers who came out for these experiences enjoyed learning how origami broke down complex ideas into simple actions and found insights to bring into their day-to-day.

This was my first hint that origami had more to teach me, and others, about the intricacies of visual communication, instructional design and more. The enthusiasm of the groups I was teaching kept me inspired to do more.

An Experience is Worth a Thousand Slides

When I started teaching design thinking to groups and organizations in 2012, I was obsessed with getting people to open up, have fun, and take a more experimental approach to their work. Teaching through improv games was attractive to me and the results were good but I wanted more. I wanted people to get under the hood and really experience what design thinking was about.

I never liked teaching in a dark, sleepy room with a group of people sitting in one direction, facing me, watching slides. When Michael taught origami it was fun, funny, and engaging. In the one day design thinking bootcamp I co-designed and taught regularly at the Design Gym, the prototyping phase of design thinking came after lunch and people clearly needed an energy boost. I needed something extra.

One day, I had an inspiration.

"Grab a piece of paper" I said, "and close your eyes. We're going to make an origami elephant in 30 seconds!"

The origami exercise helped me make my lesson in prototyping tactile and immediate instead of theoretical and distant. It's like how a picture is worth a thousand words. But in this case, an experience is worth a thousand slides. I started to wonder how I could use paper to illuminate other lessons of Design Thinking.

Who Can Use This Book

If you teach design thinking to teams, you might enjoy pulling some of these exercises into your work. That's the context that they were developed in.

You could also be an agile coach trying to unlock some creativity in a group you're working with. You might be leading a team trying to build a more innovative organization. Or you just might be a person on a team trying to get your group to think differently and to talk about how you work. If they're up for a little fun, any of these exercises can be 30-60 minutes well spent at an off site.

I've used these exercises in this book to:

Help a cross-functional team at a national bank discuss and align on what a prototype means for them. (With the 30 Second Elephant.)

Get 150 people from a distributed organization, meeting together for the first time, to talk about what good communication means. (With the Paper Airplane Experiment.)

Bring together a small UX team from a huge audio company to talk about first guesses and deepen their team cohesion. (With the Bad Guess Exercise.)

Teach facilitators at an education startup about giving clear instructions and asking better questions. (Using the Making Things Unclear Exercise.)

I've spent the last several years trying to unlock creativity and deepen collaboration in teams that were stuck. All the slides in the world wouldn't make that change. These exercises are experiences that inspire conversation while the origami makes those experiences tangible and visceral. These conversations can help shift the energy and perspectives of people.

If that sounds like something you're into, you might enjoy these exercises and this book.

How to Use this Book

This is a book of origami exercises to help explain what design means and how to collaborate with others in fresh ways.

When I talk about design, I mean a process to make things better—on purpose. Everything in our world is designed, either intentionally, or unintentionally. Making something great means you have to collaborate with other people. It's very rare to be able to bring an idea into the world without working with someone else. That collaboration might take place at the beginning, in inception, or towards the end, as you make and launch your ideas. Great things require great design. Design is how something works, not just how it looks. (Steve Jobs said that, so it *must* be true!)

The exercises in this book will help you and your team discover and master different concepts behind design thinking. Design thinking is a little different than design in that can be used by people who aren't designers to refine and deepen their ideas, and to collaborate better with professional grade designers. Anyone can use design thinking to come up with great ideas, get clearer on them, and collaborate with other people better in service of those ideas.

The Shape of Design Thinking

UK Design Council published a pretty simple diagram that summarizes a very solid perspective on design thinking: The Double Diamond.

The idea behind the double diamond is that design is a pattern of work that moves through four phases: Discovery of human needs, Defining a problem in a fresh way, Developing powerful solutions to that problem and Delivering on the promise of those solutions. It "flares" and "focuses" along the way, opening and closing options, ideas and narratives.

The way I draw the double diamond is to include a tiny dot, all the way to the left. That dot is a question, an itch, that moves us into action. An amazing question is like rocket fuel, moving people forward with clarity. To **Discover** what a problem is about you need to look at it with fresh eyes. Chapter One outlines and unpacks an exercise I use to help people rethink how they facilitate teams clearly and guide people through this complexity. While you might, as a leader, feel you know the right approach, people need to discover their own path. Facilitating that process is about asking better questions and guiding people to be open to hearing unexpected answers. **The Blind Origami Exercise** can help your team talk through these challenges. Your team will also learn how hard it can be to get on the same page without your eyes open!

Discovery is about being open to fresh ways of looking at a challenge. But eventually we all need to **Define** it in a shared way: How are we going to approach our challenge together? Chapter Two, **The Airplane Experiment**, helps people see how crucial it is to rethink how we approach defining challenges collaboratively. The Airplane Experiment can also teach teams about how design thinking isn't a linear process as the UK Design Council diagrams it. I use this exercise to show people how prototyping and testing (developing and delivering) can happen in surprisingly fast and iterative ways. If you want your team to get closer to their customers more often, this exercise is a gem!

Once we've got a good idea of how to solve a challenge, how do we **Develop** it and start to bring it to life? Chapter Three's **30 Second Elephant** is a fun exercise that helps people rethink the idea of prototyping. Ideas have lots of dimensions, and we can't bring them all to life at once - that would take too long! Finding the core, the gesture, the essence of an idea makes it a lot easier to prototype.

Delivering on the promise of an idea can feel like a lot of pressure - we want to get it right, right? But that's not the design thinking way. Chapter Four is about learning to worry less about how close to perfection your idea can be and more about the iterations that come after. **Make, Test, Reflect** can help your team see that the first draft doesn't matter...it's about a feedback loop once your idea is in the world. Hopefully, with a more mindful approach to work, your output will feel like an exclamation point!

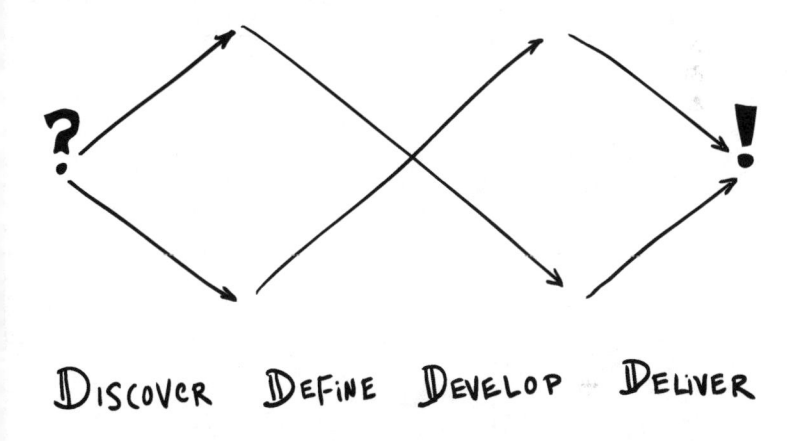

Discover   Define   Develop   Deliver

Don't *Just* Read This Book

What? Don't read the book I just started reading?

If you just read the words on these pages, you may find that the book will introduce you to some interesting concepts. It will be a mindful and reflective experience on the world around you.

BUT what I recommend is taking out a sheet of paper and actually trying these exercises with other people. The facilitation of the exercises within a team or group of people can create a space for much needed conversation.

This book is a conversation. These exercises will reveal habits and ways of thinking you and your team might not even be aware of and give you the tools to think more clearly together.

No shopping trips required: Just Paper

You may have come across the Marshmallow Challenge. If you haven't, give it a google, watch a video on YouTube or the TED talk about it. It's a great exercise...I've seen people lead it and spark amazing conversations. But I don't want to have to go to the supermarket each time I want to teach a team about being customer-centric, or about leadership, or teamwork.

I spent years running around New York City with giant tote bags of sticky notes and sharpies teaching workshops at the Design Gym. I had no time to add a bag of marshmallows, a box of spaghetti and a roll of tape to the shopping list. I like a more stripped-down approach. That's where I turned to my old friend, origami!

The exercises in this book are something you can do anytime, anywhere, with any team you want to help to collaborate, communicate, and design better.

All you need is regular printer paper, nothing else.

Out of the Perpetual Loop

I believe design is important in all aspects of life. The principles extracted from the exercises here can be applied to so many different facets of our everyday lives.

One of the things you'll hear me say over and over in this book is that you need to think about your thinking. Or in other words, challenge what you automatically perceive about the world around you. If you and I don't stop to reflect and ask some of these questions, we fall into a loop of habit.

What's so bad about that? Well...if we work habitually, fresh ideas will never stand a chance. We can't solve the deeply pressing issues of the world with the same thinking we used to create them. We need to break the loop.

These different exercises will ask you to stop and reflect. You'll be able to focus on questions like: What's working in how we work? What needs to change and why? How is our team communicating and how could it be better? Are we inviting diversity of thought into our process? And more questions that I can't even guess at. Each exercise is a tactile, open-ended experience and your mileage will vary. The more open you and your team are as you explore these exercises, the more you'll get out of them. There's no "right" experience to be had from them, just a conversation worth having.

While going through the book, I've approached each exercise in four pieces:

1. A short essay that puts the exercise into context: the history of the exercise, where I stole it, or how it was inspired and evolved.
2. The origami exercise outlined in simple steps. You only need paper for these exercises. Well, paper and people: remember, you *can* read this book alone, but the exercises come alive in discussion with other people.
3. Several pages "unpacking" each exercise. When I'm teaching teams about design thinking, I might pull out a couple of key points or turn the unpacking into a mini-lecture or a longer group discussion. These pages summarize interesting ideas to highlight and discuss.
4. A summary of key points about the exercise and the design principles I want people to walk away from the exercise understanding, knowing, and believing. A one-pager, if you will. I find people like those.

These exercises were firstly designed for facilitating within teams. I use these exercises when I'm teaching teams design thinking, user experience design, and facilitation as well as creative leadership. In a broader context, the exercises are for those who want to think differently and have a deep conversation about how they communicate, collaborate, and create together.

I've taught them at organizations like Capital One, Accenture, and Pandora, and creative agencies like Edelman, Razorfish, and Moment. They're industrial grade exercises, tested and tried. Recently, I ran into a senior creative director who was at one of these sessions. We recognized each other, even though our workshop was several years ago. He said to me "I still use the tools from that session, every day."

If you want to teach your team a fresh way of thinking, in a way that makes a real impact, you don't have to fly a facilitator in—you can just try one of these exercises. I mean, if you want to fly me in, that's cool, too.

Redesign Your Conversations

Collaboration and communication are the building blocks of work and life. These skills are critical day to day, all the time. If you're into the idea of shaping and transforming conversations, you might want to geek out with me on my podcast, The Conversation Factory.

The lessons I've learned from talking to conversation designers of all stripes have shaped the ideas in this book, so if you want to check out the source material, head over to www.TheConversationFactory.com and dig in.

Speaking of digging in...let's get into it, shall we?

CHAPTER ONE

BLIND ORIGAMI:
How might we ask the right question?

It's hard to resist a generous question. —Krista Tippet

When I was six-years-old, my dad took me to the Museum of Natural History in New York to see the Origami Holiday Tree. They had tables nearby where volunteers would teach kids a few models. (A decade later I'd be back, teaching kids, continuing the cycle!) That was my first introduction to the art of paperfolding. I was hooked. But it wasn't until I was 12 or 13 that I really started to geek out on it. I was lucky enough to get apprenticed to an origami master, who just happened to be neighbors with my mom's best friend. Michael Shall was one of the US's first full-time origami professionals. I'd follow him around the city as best I could; he had calves of steel from rollerskating in the park and climbing the five flights to his NYC studio. I had to walk as fast as I could to keep up with him.

In the summer, he would teach origami to groups of kids at public libraries around the city. One summer day I found myself in a giant room filled with 50 kids, all rapt with attention. Michael wasn't a commanding presence because he was tall (he wasn't.) Michael commanded attention in a room with his big, clear, paced voice.

"In school when you copy from someone's paper it's called cheating. In origami it's called sharing!" Michael said to the students. Chuckles moved through the room like a ribbon. With one simple phrase he gave the entire room permission to think together. His message was clear: you don't have to struggle alone, just look up and around if you're confused.

Every model starts out easy. Fold in half, unfold. A few steps in, things get a bit more challenging and the noise in the room gradually increases. I could hear the buzz of thinking brains and moving hands folding the paper. Kids would look around to check their work and the room would settle down again. If the noise kept going, rising, Michael had another move to get things back on track. He would stop, hold up his model up so everyone could see it, and tell the room, "Show me what I'm showing you!"

In a moment the room was filled with 50 kids holding their origami models high in the air. At a glance, Michael could see what was happening in the room. Were students behind? Did someone miss a fold? And everyone was focused, ready for the next step. Instruction, action, confirmation. He kept us all together.

After surveying the room he would help the kids who were struggling, tell them to copy from a neighbor, or send me over to help them fix their model. I was never allowed to touch their paper, though (that would defeat the point - they had to learn, to do it themselves.) I could only help by asking them better questions.

With his masterful instructions, there wasn't much for me to do, frankly. Michael was leading us all to a place of clarity and unity. We would *all* make a bunny rabbit and we would *all* get there painlessly!

Lockstep or Freeform?

Michael was a wizard at getting a whole room moving in unison, in lockstep towards a clear goal. Most of the organizations I work with know that to move towards innovation, growth, and transformation, the lockstep approach has to change. Top-down working, command and control, isn't the way forward. But then again, neither is total freeform chaos. What's in the middle?

We still want to be moving in the same direction, playing by the same rules but must balance our desired outcome of innovation and variety, not lockstep unity. In that case, we need to make our instructions more open-ended. An innovation culture has to blend clarity and confusion delicately.

A Shared Vocabulary

Everything Michael said was crisp and clear. No words lacked meaning. "Fold this over there," is a vague set of instructions that leads to confusion—something Michael would never let happen. "Fold the raw edge to the bottom right hand corner making a crisp crease," is a precise, purposeful instruction.

Michael built our shared vocabulary slowly and organically. The first time he said, "raw edge," he defined it as the cut edge of the paper. He spoke clearly, used the word in context, and made sure the students understood. Pretty soon the whole room was fluent in "origami."

When I began to teach facilitation I wanted to share some of the magic Michael taught me about leading a room. Origami seemed like the perfect way to show people how unclear facilitation leads to frustration. I paired Michael's communication expertise with a thought exercise from my friend David Lister to show how different ways of communicating brings different results. David was a grand old British gentleman who collected origami oddities. I met him when I was 16 at the British Origami Society's 25th anniversary convention in London. You'll learn more about him later!

This exercise has the tendency to annoy some people because we're all trained from an early age to get things right and to assume there's always a right answer. We also often assume that the right answer will always come from the front of the room, especially in cultures that have punished people for independent thinking in the past. We learn to be quiet and wait to "just be told what to do." This next exercise plays with all those expectations.

Blind Origami: Exercise Steps

1. Get a group of people together that you'd like to confuse and give them all a piece of paper. (Regular printer paper is fine.)
2. Ask them to close their eyes.
3. Tell them, "Fold your paper in half."
4. When they ask, "Which way?" ignore them.
5. Tell them, "Fold a corner down."
6. Repeat Step 4.
7. Say, "Pleat the other corner."
8. Repeat Step 4.
9. Tell them to open their eyes and ask, "What happened?"
    Answers may include:
    Frustration, chaos, mess.
10. Ask, "What could have made that experience better?

Unfolding the Exercise: What Are You Communicating?

The first instruction was to fold the paper in half. There are several common ways to fold a piece of paper in half, all of them correct. More surprising, the number of ways to divide a piece of paper into two equal areas is actually infinite! Three are shown below: Two folds you know, the third will leave some participants incredulous. (I had to prove this third way really worked during a facilitation intensive at a PR agency.) The idea that there was an infinite number of ways to do the first instruction correctly was shocking! The implications on everyday communication were sobering, to say the least.

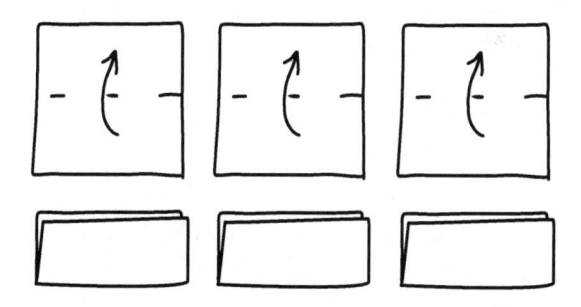

At the very least, it's worth stepping back and thinking about how you, as a leader, could be misunderstood. It's worth realizing that there are many ways to meet the challenge you're laying out.

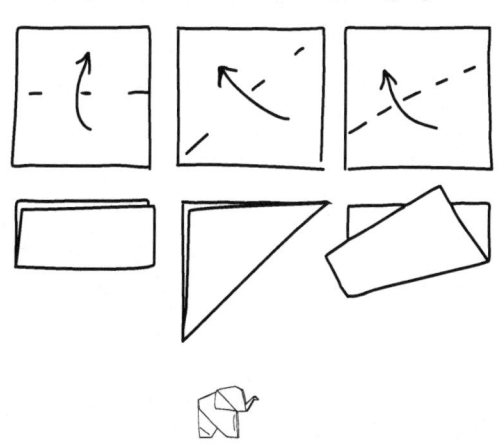

Opening More lines of Communication

One of the most common answers to the question, "What could have made that experience better?" is "We could have had our eyes open." This answer is more profound than most people realize. If we're collaborating in the same room, it's actually the easiest modality possible. We can see the same things, hear the same things, and can talk in real time. We have words, eye contact, body language, and written sticky notes. It's a multi-channel communication.

So much of work is done remotely now, and our communication channels get fragmented and asynchronous. How can we "open our eyes" and add more channels, and sync them up in our work? It's question with no easy answer, but one I love using this exercise to get people to explore together.

Open & Closed Instructions Set Different Expectations

I first used this exercise to teach people what it meant to give clear instructions as a facilitator. When I'm directing a group through a series of exercises I need to be extremely clear about certain things. On one hand, I need to make it clear that I want people to use a specific color of post-it note, size of paper, or pen when it matters to the exercise. I close out or narrow down options, on purpose. Other times, I give a more broad or general instruction like "draw your job." I leave the instructions open, because I want people to feel free to capture anything. I don't want to limit their approach.

In this exercise, my open instructions created tension in the room. What if I had said, "Whatever you do with the paper is fine. We're just experimenting to see what you get. Fold it as you feel"? The group would have felt a lot happier with the uncertainty. By setting those clear intentions, people wouldn't end up as frustrated.

Open instructions invite diversity. Closed instructions encourage consistency. Leaders and facilitators need to find a balance between the two. Most often, I find leaders use closed instructions more than than they intend to and that facilitators leave things open unintentionally. Thinking through how you might be misunderstood is helpful.

Before giving instructions, starting a project, or communicating in general, it's important to ask yourself a few questions:

- What do I want? What's my goal?
- What are the expectations of my team?
- How can I communicate my goals in a way that gets to my desired outcome?
- How can I communicate in a way that makes the team feel comfortable and engaged?

Simple, right? Yet so much stress comes from people missing the mark on this!

What kind of help do you need from people? How can you ask in a way to get that participation?

The Innovation Challenge: Balancing Diversity and Uniformity

In many large companies, uniformity is what their success is built on. When leadership says they want innovation, diversity of experimentation, people are stuck relying on uniformity. They want to be told exactly how to do it! This is one reason a standardized approach to design thinking can be so attractive. How can leadership manage clarity of direction and purpose with an openness of approach?

We need a variety of ideas in order to hope for a good one and we need ideas that are all heading towards a shared goal. This is the challenge of every innovation project and every leader of a team that needs to drive innovation: We don't want random ideas, we want ideas that solve a crucial challenge. We need unity in purpose but also need diversity in methods or approach.

Ask Generous Questions

If you want new or fresh ideas, you need to invite that by asking questions that allow generous and creative results. There's energy in inviting people into a project focused on innovation and ideas. Asking a "generous question" invites energy in kind. The bigger the question, the more energy you can get from your team. I'll give an example.

Defining Terms: What does "Impact" Mean?

Just like Michael did, we need to define a shared vocabulary if we're going to move forward together. I recently facilitated an event for a large financial company that wanted to help improve the lives of female entrepreneurs as part of their corporate social responsibility initiatives. A team of 20 high performers in the organization spent two days in an intense workshop that I co-led. We had interviews with real women from the community who were building businesses. We sketched, ideated, and built several concepts that were shared with some senior executives in the organization. After the dust settled, the head of innovation asked me, "How can we take these ideas and combine them into one really awesome idea to share with the CEO? What should we launch?"

After asking a few more questions, it turned out that the CEO had asked them to give her one idea that met three specific criteria... that were never explained to the people in the workshop (or to me!) She wanted an idea that would have "impact, splash, and signature." The head of innovation explained his understanding of the definitions:

Impact meant the measurable change could be seen in the lives of women entrepreneurs.

Splash meant something that would generate PR for the company.

Signature meant that it was something that was potentially "ownable" for the organization and not easily copied by others.

The challenge statement for the workshop was, "How might we transform the lives of female entrepreneurs?" It was a great challenge question. One that the workshop lead had spent significant time with the innovation group honing. It empowered the workshop participants to explore things broadly and to respond to whatever they learned from the interviews. The workshop teams came up with several great ideas, just maybe not ones that met the criterion of the CEO. Oops.

One group came up with an idea that followed a small cohort of female entrepreneurs and supported them in a deep, lasting way, over a year. The other group came up with an idea that would help the lives of potentially thousands of different entrepreneurs on a more shallow scale, with a downloadable toolkit and an app linking to resources. So which one had more impact? Was it about the number of women helped or the depth to which the women were helped? I didn't know and neither did the head of innovation! Wouldn't it have been awesome for the CEO to have explained her goals and how she defined "impact" so that all of the ideas at the end of the two days were in line with that view?

Asking Better Questions is the Answer

How could asking a better question have helped the situation? Should we have defined the goal more clearly? Or should the CEO get excited about some of the ideas that expand the terms of the debate?

If we define the question tightly, we get what we want—and that's good. But we might miss out on something surprising. Would a tighter, more closed question have generated as much energy and enthusiasm? I think it's possible to find that balance. We have to! For real innovation we need a balance of open and closed questions.

What I learned from Michael, was that in order for successful models to be made, terms needed to be clear and understood by everyone involved. You need to build a shared vocabulary. He would always explain what a "raw edge" was so we could fold it to lie along the center crease. The CEO needed an origami lesson before she commissioned the workshop challenge!

Four Takeaways:

1. Expect to be misunderstood. Without being specific you can get a lot of responses. Use clearer language to express intent and to anticipate how you might be (mis)understood.

2. Balance diversity and uniformity. It's okay to have a unity of purpose and a diversity of method. Make sure you are clear in communicating which you are looking for: lots of really different ideas or a few that are similar in crucial ways.

3. Define terms. When you are measuring a design or idea against certain criteria be sure to define these terms and values beforehand to your team.

4. Ask more generous questions. Spend time to craft questions that inspire innovation and creativity. Then, prepare to be surprised!

CHAPTER TWO

THE PAPER AIRPLANE EXPERIMENT

Communicate and Collaborate Better Together

> *The biggest problem in communication is the illusion it has taken place. —George Bernard Shaw*

When I was making the transition from Industrial Design to User Experience Design around 2008, I noticed that the way UX designers communicate their ideas was a lot like how origami was diagrammed. In UX it's called wireframing and in origami it's called the Yoshizawa-Randlett system. The Yoshizawa-Randlett system is why I can read an origami book in any language. The author has taken the time to break down their ideas into small, clear steps. Wireframing design tries to do the same thing...but the process is tedious, and is often easy to misunderstand. Breaking down a digital interaction into tiny steps gets exhausting. While origami diagrams are for finished ideas, wireframes are used for ideas in all stages of development.

What's the point of documenting ideas in exhaustive detail if they might not work in real life? This exercise explores that tension, between clarity of communication and quality of ideas.

In 2010, I got my first senior UX role at a small company, and I thought it would be fun to teach my UX team some origami, so they could learn a different perspective on visual clarity and communication. It was a hit with the team, and I went on to teach this exercise at several other top UX agencies like Moment and Razorfish and at public workshops, too. I later developed this exercise as the backbone of an introductory UX bootcamp I taught at General Assembly in New York. Over several years of teaching that workshop, I refined this exercise to tune people into the nuances of communication at all stages of an idea.

The Paper Airplane Experiment has evolved over time as it's passed through the hands of different people. For example, my friend Carl Collins suggested an additional twist at the end that you'll see later. It's now a core part of how I run it.

Good on Paper

When you fall in love with an idea, it seems perfect in your head. Getting that idea into someone else's head intact...that's a bigger challenge! Putting it on paper takes time and in that time, we only fall in love with our idea more. Sometimes this is called "The Ikea Effect." I've seen it illustrated as the Love/Time axis, drawn below.

It can be dangerous falling in love with our ideas before they reach the real world. Even more frustrating is when we take time to craft and explain our idea and it's not understood by the people on the other side.

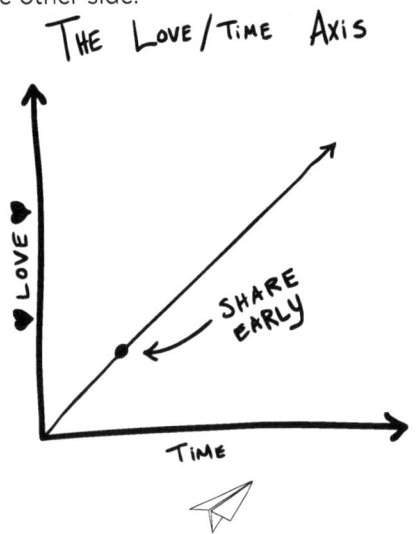

The Love/Time Axis

In organizations I work with, this looks like an ever growing and refining powerpoint deck. The deck will explain all.

But then sometimes your share your idea, your deck...and there's a big gap. They just don't get it. Which is crazy, given how great your idea AND your deck explaining it are!

This Love/Time Axis can be dangerous. My solution: get it out of your head and into the real world as quickly as possible, while you can still be clear-eyed about it!

How did we decide? Who is it for?

Years ago, I was working with a big pharmaceutical company on a device redesign. We took months to develop our plans to revamp the system, in coordination with our key client stakeholder, and crafted a beautiful, glossy, giant poster of the new system architecture and printed it out six feet square and tacked it on the wall. We intended to use this poster in a workshop with the broader team to share our roadmap.

The sheer glossy perfection of the map made the CEO and executive team look at it and say, "that looks expensive."

We had created a great visual of the system but quickly realized something was missing. There was a disconnect between the final presentation and the process that brought us to decide that this was the right way forward. We had to clarify what problem we were solving for their customers and we should have done it sooner, in a much, much less glossy way. While we had every intention that this diagram would help facilitate a conversation, it did the opposite and actually scared the stakeholders.

It's easy to focus on how wonderful our own ideas are but in order to communicate these ideas to others well, it's important to step back and "show your work." How do we communicate our process and answer questions like, "How did you decide this option? What makes it the best way forward...and for who?"

This exercise is to help you avoid these situations—or rather, experience them faster and purposefully while learning from them. Never overbuild to communicate again! Never fall in love with your idea before testing it!

Communicating In Teams

I've worked with teams and organizations on how to work together, better, all over the world. All of the challenges teams come up against when they are trying to innovate come down to a lack of clear communication. Without clear communication, great collaboration is impossible.

This is an exercise I facilitate with teams who want to work in the same direction at the same time, instead of pulling in different directions. If your team wants more positive collaboration, try this out. The whole exercise with discussions can take less than an hour, depending on the size of your group.

The Paper Airplane Experiment: Exercise Steps

1. Get a group of people together and pair everyone up (threes are fine, too.)
2. Ask each group to "make a set of instructions on how to make a paper airplane."
3. Set the timer for 10 minutes.
4. Talk about what you made: What ways of explaining your work did you use?
5. Talk about how you chose which airplane to make.
6. Swap instructions with another team and try them out. Which methods worked well? Which fell flat? Did you get the plane you intended?

Unfolding the Exercise: Collaborating in Teams

At the end of the ten minutes, almost every team will come up with a different set of instructions for their paper airplane. And many will have a different plane. Their overt goal was to make instructions, and the secret goal of the exercise is to get participants to examine the way they decide on what to make. I want people to examine how they decide, not just how they communicate what they decide.

We'll get your team to unpack the deeper question of how they make group decisions, but I find starting with the what and getting to the why is easier!

Explaining Your Plane

My first unpacking question is simple: "What did you make?"

I want to see what each team did and why. After years of running this experiment, it's clear that "instructions" must look like numbered steps written down on a piece of paper.

50% of teams that participate in the exercise will create "one-dimensional directions," meaning they used just words. One person will fold and verbally explain the process to another person, who writes it all down, just like a business analyst recording requirements from a stakeholder.

Some teams will use symbols and diagrams to go along with the written directions, making the communication "two-dimensional" and removing potential ambiguity with the words.

Occasionally teams will take another approach by creating a series of three-dimensional planes. (These are called step folds, like origami breadcrumbs, and are great for blind origami instruction.) Sometimes people get clever and write their instructions directly on the folded plane. I call that "object as interface." Only by exploring the object can you figure out how to fold the plane.

One thing that I have never seen a team do is to pull out the cell phone that everyone has in their pockets and make a video of the entire process. Why? Most people fear that would be breaking the rules. The assumption that directions must be one dimensional and that thinking outside the box would be breaking the rules is so limiting to creative communication!

This goes for designing more than just paper airplanes and paper airplane directions. It's the same for designing bridges or businesses, conversations, and communities. Breaking the rules often leads to the most beautifully designed parts of life.

Once I've recorded all the ways the teams explored communicating, I'll ask, "Why did no one take a video?" Their mouths open a bit and they look collectively towards the ground. No one knows what to say and you can almost hear the inward twinge of "Why didn't we break the rules?"

One pre-reader of this book pointed out that someone could draw an airplane on paper, cut it out, and be making a "paper airplane" in a very different sense.

There are always unspoken rules and it's always worth not leaving them unspoken. After all you can't break the rules if you don't know what they are!

This way, we are able to see our natural tendency to stay within the boundaries and not question what's possible. Many of us think we're innovating and challenging but it's impossible to deny that our tendency is towards safety. This exercise illustrates in real time the choices we have and challenges us to see all the options available. It forces us to realize we must pick our options intentionally, instead of reflexively.

Best How? For Who?

Which type of visual communication is the best? The answer is always, it depends. Videos seem like a great idea (that we wish we'd thought of!) but they only work when I have electricity or internet. Words with pictures might be great unless you're blind.

Who are these instructions for? We never asked! So many organizations are locked into a "go and do" culture. Questioning the question is always a good idea. Teams will complain that I didn't give them enough time to think. But isn't that the way it is day to day? Time pressure can't be an excuse to not think.

How Did You Communicate and Decide Within Your Team?

Once we've established the variety of visual communication open to us, I get the teams to explore how they chose which plane to fold and diagram. With only ten minutes in the exercise, teams rush to get the job done. Getting them to slow down and think about how they made this choice afterwards is one of juiciest outcomes of this exercise for me.

There are a few very predictable things that happen as far as communication within the group. The most common I call: First Speaker Syndrome.

First Speaker Syndrome is when someone speaks up first and says something like, "I know a good paper airplane," and so (without question) the rest of the group goes along with the first speaker. This is a major mistake. Each person has a unique experience and perspective that could improve a project. Why not design the conversation to make sure everyone is heard before decisions are made? And ask each teammate to be aware of how they might be affecting that conversation.

Some questions worth considering for team members: Who are you within the group? Are you the person who speaks first and doesn't give time to others' ideas? Are you the person who goes along with ideas for the sake of harmony? Or are you the person pushing and challenging the group to make the best airplane there is?

With the clock ticking, the temptation to ignore ideas or not speak up in opposition is strong. But what your team does with ten minutes is often a pretty good indicator of what they'll do when the time window is longer.

When you lead this exercise, leave time for this conversation about intentional decision making to evolve. There is a lot of transformative potential in bringing awareness to this little moment, when teams go from an infinite set of possibilities to one.

The Best Plane for Who?

The question of "which plane" goes even deeper. Very occasionally, I'll see teams have to choose between two planes. How do they decide? Is the best plane the one that flies longest? Fastest? Highest? Most maneuverable? Easiest to fold? Easiest for us to diagram?! These questions almost never get asked. Why? Time. We don't take time to ask these totally critical questions...and so we spend our time designing the wrong thing, or not the best thing.

Taking a moment to think, "Why am I doing this? What's the real goal here?" is never time wasted!

Did you fly the plane?

Around 80% of people who participate in this exercise never fly their plane before diagramming it. When I ask them why they didn't try out their design first, they complain about the time. And yet...there will always be one or two groups who somehow managed to *each* fold a plane they know, try them both out, and then make diagrams for the best one. I love those teams!

Why spend ten minutes—or any time at all—designing something that doesn't even work in the end?

All Ideas are like Paper Airplanes

I'm still surprised by how many teams create directions for a paper airplane without testing if the plane even flies well. They hear the ten minute time-crunch and decide to get straight to the task: write the directions and forget who the directions are for or how clearly they communicate. Just get the job done.

Why spend even ten minutes creating detailed instructions for a paper airplane that doesn't fly? In offices everywhere, every day, people are toiling away on metaphorical paper planes that won't fly, just because they were told to.

In a broad sense, "fly" just means can it make it out of your hands and across your desk. Does the prototype you created accomplish the simple purpose of your initial design and intent? In other words, does your idea "have legs"?

A Culture of Why

All ideas are like paper airplanes. Ideas need to be tested—early and often. At the very least, they should stand the test of a simple question: Why?

Why did we choose this idea?

Why will our customer/stakeholder/client want it and need it?

Why did we choose that person as our focus?

Why do we communicate our ideas the way we do?

Why don't we try other approaches and see if they work?

Why can't we test and try our ideas sooner and get feedback on them sooner?

Remember, the first plane was not a jumbo jet. It looked more like a bicycle with wings. But it flew! Eventually it brought us to the jumbo jet we know today, one iteration at a time.

The Collins Debugging

The last step, rotating the diagrams to another team, is eye opening (and totally Carl's idea!) Watching your customers try unsuccessfully to work out your app or your stakeholder trying to decipher your deck is painful. The diagram swap emulates this reality, and I use this final round of the exercise to help people see that you can grab nearly anyone and ask them to help you "debug" your ideas.

In design thinking this is sometimes called a "think aloud test." I want people to leave the airplane experiment with some experience in the power of a quick-and-dirty test. I also want them to develop some empathy for the people who have to go through those tests! Knowing what it feels like from both sides of the table can help people do them better.

Twenty Minutes?

The other day I used this exercise as an end-of-day brain refresher with a small team I was working with to summarize a lot of the points we had worked through in our innovation process. I've also used it with 150 people over one full hour. The exercise is like water—it can fill a lot of different containers. Once you've tried it a few times, you'll find which parts are most critical to the context you're working in and focus on those.

Four Takeaways:

1. Know your audience. When you design something, keep their specific needs and desires in mind.

2. Test early and often. Incorporate a cycle of feedback so you don't end up with a finished product that doesn't fly.

3. Are you communicating what you think you're communicating? Testing your idea is one thing, testing your way of communicating is another! Do both.

4. Forgiveness over permission is always a good motto: Assume there are no rules, unless otherwise specified. The best ideas come from people and teams willing to do something in a way that hasn't been done before.

CHAPTER THREE

THE 30 SECOND ELEPHANT

What Do Prototypes Prototype?

Mock it up before you fock it up.—Bruce Hannah

When there's an idea in your head bumping around, you need to pull it out and bring it into the world to test it somehow. That's what chapter two is all about. But how do we bring an idea into the world to test it without actually making it? It's a tricky balance: make your idea in full and maybe you've wasted a lot of time in the wrong direction. But if you don't make it all the way what are you really testing anyway? That's what a prototype is all about.

I often compare big ideas to elephants. Elephants always seem to represent problems. Like the elephant in the room, it's something that needs to be figured out. In origami, elephants are challenging because they are such strangely proportioned animals. They have big legs, a big body, thin tusks, huge ears, and a little tail. That's a lot of work for one square of paper!

When I design workshops to teach non-designers the ideas of design thinking, it's to help them bring better ideas into the world, together and faster. Most of the time, everyone sees challenges differently. A group of people around an idea or problem can be like the story of the blind men and the elephant.

It's a weird story because the setup makes no sense at all! Somehow, a group of blind men are exposed to an elephant for the first time. Each feels his way over to the animal and with their sense of touch, tries to figure out what they are in contact with. Because elephants are strange, they try to interpret what they're encountering based on what they already know.

One touches the trunk and declares that it's like a great serpent!

Another feels the tail and says it's like a whip!

A third feels the tusks and says it's a stone.

And so on.

Each is right in their own way. Each is only looking at one part of the picture.

It's a silly story but ideas are really like this. We're feeling around in the dark and touch on something. Then we grab hold of it and try to figure it out. New ideas are just like elephants: everyone has their own unique perspective and sees them in different ways.

Real elephants and paper elephants are obviously two very different things. In fact, origami elephants are representations of elephants and in being representations, they strip out detail and exactness while keeping the essence, charm, and gesture of an elephant. This representation is exactly what we're looking for when we have an idea and need to create a prototype.

Origami Elephant Prototypes

There are hundreds and hundreds of different origami elephant models out there. Two of my favorites are the dollar bill elephant by John Montroll and the Baby Elephant by Fumiaki Kawahata.

The dollar bill elephant is actually pretty complete, it has a big head, tusks, a little tail, but the ears are actually just the flat of the head. Regardless, it still reads as an elephant, right?

The baby elephant is cute, simple, and doesn't have tusks or a tail, but it's still an elephant.

Baby Elephant by Fumiaki Kawahata and Dollar Bill Elephant by John Montroll

The important piece is: each model makes a choices about what to leave out and what to put in. That's the essences of a good prototype.

Rapid Prototyping

Creating a real life baby elephant takes 18-22 months, unless you factor in how long it takes to make two adult elephants who like each other and want to start a family! That's at least 2 years to sexual maturity for an elephant or 13 billion years to make an actual elephant when you factor in making a solar system, the planet for the elephant, oceans and so on. Like Carl Sagan said "If you wish to make an apple pie from scratch, you must first invent the universe." Prototyping means making things more quickly than nature...we don't have 13 billion years!

This need for speed is what led me to develop this exercise. The more quickly we can capture the essence of an idea and "give birth" to it, at least in infant form, the sooner we can get on a "Make, Test, Reflect" cycle. This exercise is about showing people how much you can do with very little time.

How can we capture the essence of elephant in just 30 seconds?

30 Second Elephant: Exercise Steps

1. Get everyone in a group with a piece of paper in hand.
2. Tell them "you're all going to make an elephant with me..." pause for dramatic effect
   " ...with your eyes closed"
   (gasps!)
   "...and in 30 seconds."
   (someone will gulp)
3. When people ask you if they are "allowed to ____" etc. Tell them that there are no more instructions.
4. "On your mark, get set...elephant!"
5. Call time at 45 seconds (I mean, 30 seconds is crazy!)
6. Ask, "What happened?"
7. Hear from some people
8. Ask people about what they made and why.

Unfolding the Exercise:
What did we make and why?

Look around the circle and have everyone else to do the same. How have they "modeled" an elephant? What have they captured and what have they left out? What "evokes" elephant in their paper models? As I look around the room, I use the lens of appreciative inquiry to find something good in every person's approach. (More on that later.)

Remember: a prototype is a representation of the thing, not the thing. Making an elephant takes 13 million years. We can make an elephant prototype in 30 seconds, only if we stick to the absolute essentials. The less you try to do, the more interesting the prototype is. If you try to make everything it's not a prototype anymore! If you act like the blind men and touch one part of it and try to make just one part of it, you can learn a lot more. And learning is the purpose of this type of prototyping!

In the dozens and dozens of times I've done this exercise in groups, I've seen some crazy strategies for elephant making, but I break them down by fundamental dimensions. I think people would do well to learn each type of prototyping, because each type can help you learn something new from your idea, each way of prototyping is like a different blind hand feeling out a part of the idea in the darkness.

Prototyping Three Ways

In my experience, there are three different levels of prototyping: Two-Dimensional, Three-Dimensional, and Four Dimensional.

Two-Dimensional Prototyping (or Drawing an Elephant)

Some people take my "no other instructions" rule at face value and grab a pen or sharpie. Still with closed eyes, they quickly sketch the outline of an elephant! I love rule benders. And I love sketchers.

Drawing is a skill that I am personally poor at but practice all the time. I compare my skills unfavorably to the people I know who are truly talented artists. But when I say "draw" as a way of prototyping an idea that can mean a lot of things, like sketching a diagram or drawing an outline of an essay.

Working out ideas with a pen and paper doesn't require any great artistic skill. Drawing makes a visual record of your thoughts over time. With those thoughts made physical, you can show them to other people, but the act of making them means you're showing the ideas to yourself! As they are unfolded to you, you respond to them. Even in drawing with yourself, there's a make, test, reflect cycle!

I try to applaud the "rule breakers" who draw an elephant...it's a good way to prototype: fast and cheap.

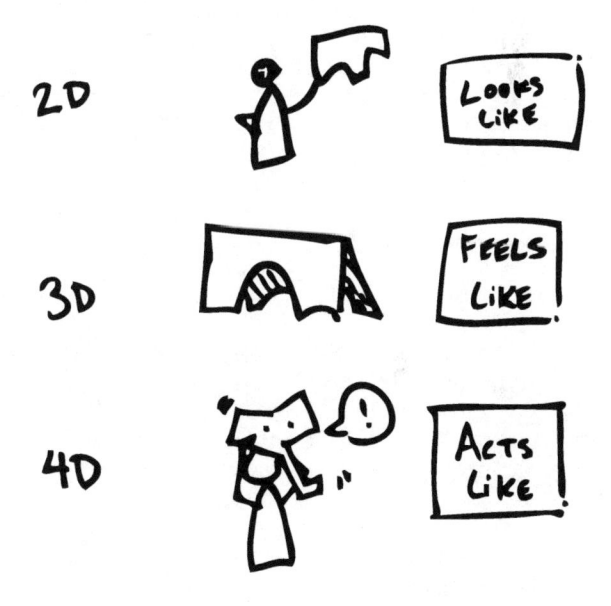

**Inspired by "What do Prototypes Prototype?"
By Stephanie Houde and Charles Hill**

Three-Dimensional Prototyping (or Folding the Elephant)

Other people fold, bend, and tear until they have a leg or two and some ears, maybe. Somehow, someone always manages to capture an elegant "gesture" or some essential "elephantine" curve. Some people capture the bulk of the elephant by folding the paper just right. They capture something in 3 dimensions that says elephant!

Some ideas are hard to explain with a drawing or difficult to work out on paper. That's when you need to use the third dimension! You know the feeling. You're trying to explain something to someone and they nod politely while you know very well they don't understand what you're actually talking to them about. Well, that's when it might be necessary to show them. Seeing is believing, right?

At my house, I have a stoop with an open area to one side where we were contemplating putting a bike storage shed. One model looked like it could fit by the side of the stoop or against an opposite wall, so I got some tape and outlined the dimensions on both sides, floors and walls, mocking up the whole shape. I was shocked to find out that one side was way too close to the door for it to work. While on the other side the steps got in the way. Using a tape measure, it looked like a fit but my 3D tape prototype revealed how much more complex the storage shed issue was! I had nearly bought it, and I was very glad I made a low-cost 3D prototype before I got too deep.

Four-Dimensional Prototyping (Imitating the Elephant)

With the added element of time, we can use a prop to show what an elephant looks, sounds, and acts like.

4D prototyping is harder to understand. I've seen someone make a trunk and tusks out of paper and stick it in their mouth in desperation as time ran out. Sitting on the table, the model is hard to understand...meaningless, even. But when a person uses it, it comes alive. 4-D prototyping can seem like a cheat: making the sounds of an elephant isn't using origami! But when you're prototyping a service or experience this approach is clutch. Sometimes this approach is called "bodystorming."

The Gesture of an Idea

What I really love about this exercise is using an Appreciative Inquiry approach to see something lovely, accurate, and redeemable in each and every elephant in the room. I take a few minutes to look around the room and find that "elephantness" in several people's models and focus on that. To me that is what a prototype is: something that captures the essence of an idea, enough to communicate it, enough to transmit the core idea without anything extra. Whether the model is 2D, 3D, or 4D, each sketch in the room is taking the idea of an elephant and stripping it down to a basic gesture. If you try to make the whole elephant, it takes 13 billion years. If you have a new elephant idea, start with the 30 second version first.

Faking an Idea to Life

Companies fake products all the time. Before they had a working technical prototype, Dropbox made an explainer video with stop-motion animated paper cut outs that helped people "get" what dropbox could do for them. The video helped Dropbox test if people felt the pain of the problem Dropbox was trying to solve.

Amazon came out with a mini handheld version of the voice agent Alexa that sticks on your fridge and can scan items to help you order them. To demonstrate the way the product works, they made a video of someone pulling the device off the fridge, opening up their fridge door, and then asking Alexa to buy more milk while scanning the label off the carton. This sort of 4D prototype doesn't require a working model, any little piece of black plastic would do...in the video there's no close up of the thing! It's the action, the voiceovers, and the element of time that makes this prototype come to life. With a bodystorming approach, you can act out how your idea will work—no coding required!

Purposeful Prototyping

Each type of prototype comes at different stages of a creative process and with different intentions behind them. I draw the diagram below for teams to illustrate the process and rings of prototyping. We all want to rush into the middle and get to a validated pilot, proof that our idea is awesome! But this is how the 20 million-dollar mistakes get made. Some VP pushes things toward the finish line, going for glory. I want teams to spend more time on the outer rings of prototyping, making their way into this juicy core!

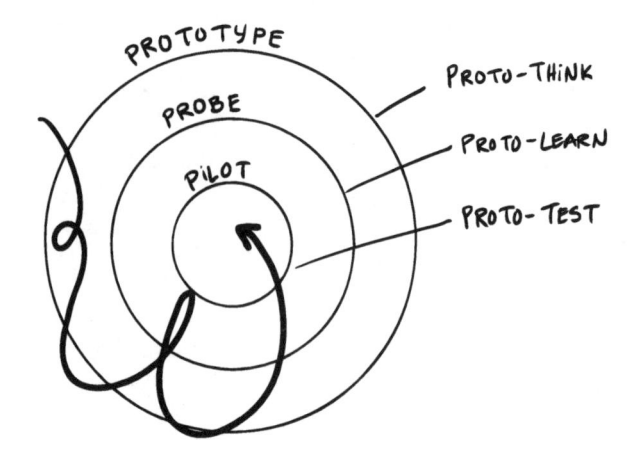

Three Modes of Prototyping

Proto-Think: a conversation with yourself to think through an idea, to see it in front of you. You learn from the *act* of making. Proto-thinking is free of charge besides time and paper.

Proto-Learn: Sharing what you've made to probe other people's reactions to your ideas. Proto-learning can cost a bit, depending on how you pay the people who try your stuff out, and what you make your sharable prototype with.

Proto-Test: Trying out your ideas in a real world setting or piloting it in some way. Proto-testing is nearly always expensive: pilots tend to take real time and money.

The bullseye diagram of the three prototyping modes is to help people see that real-world testing is earned through a process of thinking and learning, sketching and probing. It's about being intentional—deliberately earning support, feedback and momentum for your ideas.

Prototype with People

Putting something in front of an audience will help you get feedback. People can tell you how an idea feels, if it matches their mental models or lifestyle, if it works for their context, if they like how it looks, and so on. In prototyping, remember to be clear on what you're *not* prototyping to help you get more directed feedback. If you're not testing color or pricing, people might give you feedback on that anyway...which you can file away for later!

If you give people something to try out, they can only touch or feel a small part in a limited time. An hour is a lot of time to ask of someone, and you'd be surprised how few focused questions can fit into what seems like a long time. So don't bother making the whole "elephant" to the Nth degree of detail. Only make as much detail as needed to get the most critical feedback. Focusing on key components of your elephant can help you learn from people more easily.

Which Prototype to Prototype?

Knowing what "part of an idea" you're prototyping can help you to decide what type of prototype to make and how much detail to put in. There are many, many types of prototypes: storyboards, moodboards, video scenarios, business models, process maps, sketches, and physical models. All of the tools of design thinking could be seen as a prototype of one sort or another.

It's not about choosing the "right" tool. It's about choosing *a* tool and seeing what you learn from it, seeing how people interact with it, and pushing forward towards clarity.

Four Takeaways:

1. Don't try to make the whole elephant. Just make the parts that matter first.

2. Proto-think a lot before you proto-learn and proto-learn a lot before you proto-test.

3. Be clear on what your prototype is and isn't prototyping.

4. Expand your prototyping toolbox. Try new tools and see which get you more clarity, velocity, and feedback.

CHAPTER FOUR

MAKE, TEST, REFECT

The Power of Feedback Loops and Knowing When to Stop

Stay foolish. —Steve Jobs

When I was 16, my parents put me on a plane to London for my first international origami convention. I had been going to the Origami USA annual conference for four years running and folding origami obsessively since I was six and first folded under the origami tree at the Museum of Natural History in New York.

My parents were so supportive of my hobby that they let me take off school and volunteer to help set up before the NYC conventions. They were also cool with me spending the three days of the conference up until all hours of the night hanging out with other origami nerds from all over the world! It was the best vacation a nerdy kid could have ever asked for.

When I found out I was headed to the British Origami Society 25th anniversary convention I was stoked. I even had a model accepted into the program which meant I got to lead a session and teach people some of my original origami designs.

There are several things that stuck with me from the conference. The first being that English Breakfasts are gross. (Sorry England.) I really don't understand roasted tomatoes and beans and I don't think I ever will. Eggs usually help everything but in this case... not so much.

The other thing that stuck with me was a class taught by David Lister, a grand old English gentleman who loved the history of origami and collecting origami oddities. He taught me about odd folds (literally) and the power of a guess. The exercise that follows was a math oddity of his, adapted to my own purposes.

Normally, guessing and origami don't have a lot to do with one another. Most origami is like a math equation that builds on itself...and if you get one fold wrong, the foundation is off, and it's harder to find where to make the next crease. Layers slip and misalign...and then you're screwed.

Folding a piece of paper in half is hard to mess up, and that's pretty much always the first step in any origami model. Some origami models, though, start elsewhere—in thirds, fifths, sevenths, and even ninths. There are a lot of different methods people use to get to these odd divisions. Some can be slightly annoying. Most are hard to remember because they have no logic to them. And you have to remember a method for each odd division! One for thirds, another for fifths, another for sevenths. Ugh. David taught me a better way. And in the spirit of mathematical elegance, he had just *one* method for any odd division. The process started with a simple guess.

The guess didn't even have to be good. After the guess, an exponential feedback loop would make your guess accurate within the thickness of a piece of paper in just a few folds.

#nerdgasm

Start Fast and Make it Better Faster

Most organizations set a very high bar to jump over before they deem an idea "safe to try," with good reason. Companies want to stay in business and not mess up whatever good thing they have going. However, when organizations start to think about being more innovative, this "high bar" mentality can create a lot of friction. How can you get nay-sayers to be yay-sayers? This quick exercise can help break the ice on a critical concept.

What this exercise does is demonstrate how the *worst* guess can get better fast with a good feedback loop. And how we can make better guesses by looking differently. This exercise is totally impossible to get without folding it so I'll say it again: DON'T READ THIS BOOK. Take a piece of paper out and fold along.

The Lister Method for Folding Thirds

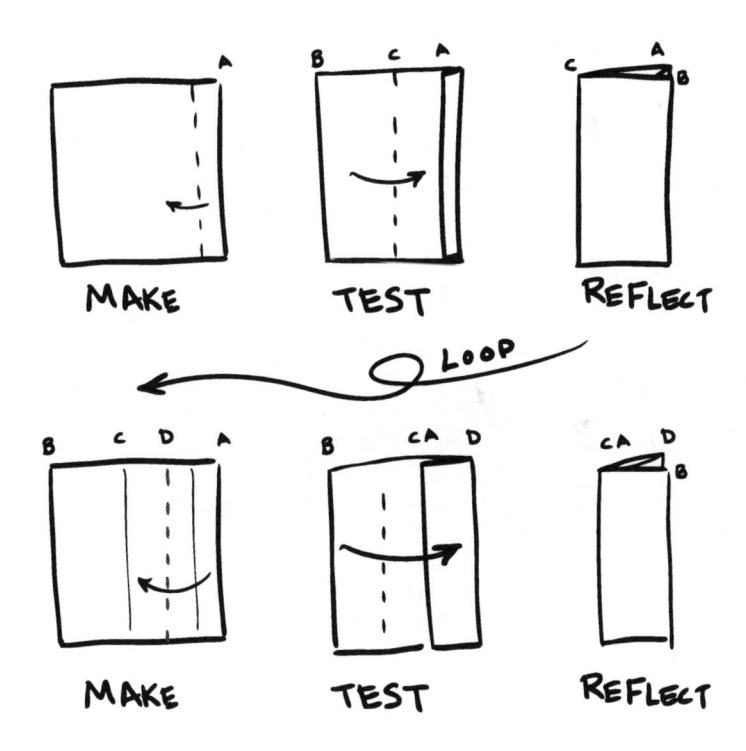

MAKE   TEST   REFLECT

LOOP

MAKE   TEST   REFLECT

The Make-Test-Reflect Exercise Steps

1. Hand out paper to your group.
2. Ask them to fold one side of the paper over about 1/3. Ask them to make the worst guess they can.
3. Assume this guess is correct and fold the opposite side to the folded edge you've just made - this is your first approximation of thirds. Then unfold.
4. Assume your last crease is correct and fold the original side to this crease.
5. Ask, "What's happening?" Pause for reflection and discussion.
6. Keep making guesses with opposing sides of the paper until your creases get so close together you can't tell them apart.

To discuss:
- Ask, "How could we make a better guess for 1/3 from the beginning? What would it look like?" Pause for reflection and discussion.
- "What does this mean for how we want to work in the future?"
- "How can we make a better guess to start off using principles discussed in the first question?"

PS - You can try this exercise with fifths (if you're feeling frisky.)

Unfolding the Exercise: Your First Draft Doesn't Matter—Mathematically

What people notice first in this exercise is how quickly even the worst guess gets very very good, very very fast. Having a good feedback loop is much more critical than having a good first guess. I could go into the math of how the feedback loop works in this exercise, but that's less important than getting people to see that iteration is the key to excellence.

Once people grasp that idea, I like pointing out that even a bad guess is better than no guess. Even the worst guess, even folding the paper in half, can get us on the path forward. It's about getting off the starting block. You can test and reflect on your first bad draft *only* if you have a draft to work with!

No Guess is Zero Percent Right

Maybe that's a weird way to put it? What I mean is that if you folded a tiny, tiny strip or a half (which is totally and completely not a third!) it's still not entirely off, mathematically. We can calculate the percent difference between our first guess and the "right answer" and I find that encouraging. A half is only 40% different from a third. Not 100% wrong...a little bit right!

The greatest part of this little origami thought experiment is that making bad guesses is scalable—this method works with fifths, sevenths, and ninths too. I like having a model that works in all cases. And in my opinion, having a defined, mutually agreed on, Make, Test, Reflect Cycle with your team is essential. And it can apply to any problem you might have.

Where is perfectionism keeping you and your team from learning and accelerating?

Test and Reflect

For my origami needs the goal is to get to equal thirds, which wrap edge to edge perfectly, like a cosy burrito. After making two creases, we should be able to check if we're on track or off track. Make, Test...and Reflect!

After each set of creases, we can step back and ask: Is it doing what it's supposed to do? The key concept here is to not judge a first guess harshly. It's about reflecting after a cycle of work. It's up to each of us to decide on how and when to test our ideas, and how to reflect on how those ideas performed.

I know: This might seem obvious to you...after all, it's the essence of the agile process, the scientific method. Yet, teams and organizations struggle with staying true to a sprint, or being honest with their starting hypotheses. It's easy to get impatient for perfection, pulling the plug on a concept before it can find it's legs. So as fundamental as these ideas are, it's nice to know that there's an origami demonstration that can put them in stark relief.

Let's Go to McDonald's: The Power of a Bad Idea

Here is a quick story about the power of bad ideas.

It's lunchtime and the someone from your group says, "What should we do for lunch?"

What follows might be silence. Or "How about Thai?" "No, I had that last week." And an endless stream of back and forth, with no progress. Maybe something similar has happened to you, too?

My friend Steve Portigal, an ace design researcher, has a method to break the deadlock:

Steve says, "Let's get McDonald's!"

One of two things will happen: either agreement or total and utter rejection.

"No, something healthy!" Someone might say.

Either way, we have movement, instead of a stalemate.

A bad guess gets you off the starting block and into the process of improvement. This exercise puts this fact into your hands clearly. It's a worthwhile conversation to have with your team.

A great question to ask your team: "How bad can our guesses be when we get started? How can we give ourselves permission to start? How can we create cycles of making, testing, and reflection that works for our context? How can they be faster?"

When do we stop learning and start launching?

David Lister's method, in essence, is to build off of each guess, to keep learning. And each loop of learning, each iteration gets us closer to perfect. I want to show you a little more math, just for fun. If you were to make your first fold a half, you're 40% off the mark. A second guess with the Lister method gets you a fourth, which is 28% off the mark. A third, and a fourth iteration gets us closer and closer. Pretty quickly, though, the rate of improvement flattens out and it becomes a game of inches. How good does it need to be? How do we know when to stop?

With origami, the stopping point is obvious: the thickness of the paper steps in and the creases get so close together you can't tell them apart. You know you can't go any further. In innovation, it can be harder to see when it's time to stop iterating and testing and time to go raise some VC money!

Perfect is the Enemy

Design isn't about making it right the first time. It's about making a bad first draft, testing it, reflecting, and then doing it again. Dave Lister taught me that an estimate and a process of continuous improvement was better than a grab bag full of "perfect" methods.

I hope this exercise has opened your mind to the possibility that a good cycle of reflection and revision means you can get better even if you aren't good from the start.

The first thing you do doesn't have to be perfect. The last iteration won't be perfect, either. Just good enough to get going with.

I see a lot of teams where the barrier to action is so high—and it makes me sad because you have to prove everything to everyone to the Nth degree before you get any real feedback, where the magic really is. It's common in many organizational cultures that projects and ideas need to be perfectly thought out before you let them out the door.

Look before you Crease!

While this exercise teaches the power of a bad guess, it's also useful in teaching the idea of making better guesses. We accomplished all these folds by making two bad guesses in the very beginning, but an educated guess can get you there even faster.

Looking at the problem differently, stepping back and reflecting *before* you make your first really dumb guess, isn't a bad idea. The first crease of folding thirds should actually look like this:

Notice that the folded side on the right and the area on the left are the same width? That's because a half of a third is a third. I use this method when I fold odd divisions to make my first estimate really good because I'm looking before creasing!

It's kind of like watching elbows when executing a high five...it's much more reliable than watching the hand. Folding a third is hard. But with this method of looking, I'm actually making two equal areas. Somehow that's easier to do.

How can flipping your challenge on it's head help you make a better guess? What aren't you measuring or tracking that you could?

Four Takeaways:

1. A bad guess is better than no guess. In this origami experiment, the worst guess is still better than a coin toss odds. Our second guess winds up being even better. Making it moves the conversation forward.

2. Test your guess. How should it act? Does your guess act like it should? Any good hypothesis has testable implications. Think on those and look for signs.

3. Have a feedback loop and iterate. Reflect on how to take what you now know and feed it back into your process. Your guesses will get better even faster, even if they're never perfect.

4. Look before you crease! Reframe the problem or step back from the challenge to look at it a different way and make more awesome guesses.

CONCLUSION

FINAL THOUGHTS

I hope you enjoyed reading through these exercises and even more, I hope you took some time to try one (or more) of them.

As I assembled this book, I realized that these exercises are connected more than I thought. Each lesson is part of my philosophy of design thinking: Start Small, Make Things, Collaborate Deeply, Ask Amazing Questions. With some effort, you can sprinkle small pieces of design thinking throughout your days and shift your world significantly.

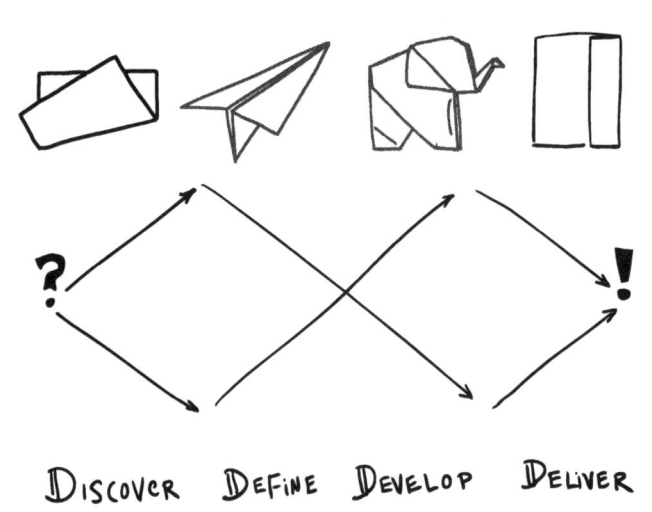

Discover   Define   Develop   Deliver

Where can you take an opportunity to make an educated (or miseducated) guess on something? Where can you reach outside of your own expectations to ask for the right types of feedback?

Where can you find a way to collaborate with others to find the right question to ask? How can you think about being misunderstood in a positive way?

All of these exercises are designed to help people step back and reflect:

How do we work today?
How is that working?
How can we make it work better?
How can we start that change?

Your ideas and life will be better the more you ask these questions and do something with the answers!

Made in the USA
Lexington, KY
21 July 2019